Young woman playing a
clavichord (painting attributed
to Jan van Hemessen, Flemish,
1500-66).

THE BOOK OF THE PIANO
An Illustrated History

By Dr. Mark Zilberquit
Translated from the Russian by Yuri S. Shirokov

PUBLISHED BY PAGANINIANA PUBLICATIONS, INC.
P.O. Box 427, Neptune, N.J. 07753
Manufactured in the U.S.A.

Distributed in the UNITED STATES by T.F.H. Publications, Inc., 211 West Sylvania Avenue, Neptune City, NJ 07753; in CANADA to the Book Trade by Macmillan of Canada (A Division of Canada Publishing Corporation), 164 Commander Boulevard, Agincourt, Ontario M1S 3C7; in ENGLAND by T.F.H. Publications Limited, 4 Kier Park, Ascot, Berkshire SL5 7DS; in AUSTRALIA AND THE SOUTH PACIFIC by T.F.H. (Australia) Pty. Ltd., Box 149, Brookvale 2100 N.S.W., Australia; in NEW ZEALAND by Ross Haines & Son, Ltd., 18 Monmouth Street, Grey Lynn, Auckland 2, New Zealand; in SINGAPORE AND MALAYSIA by MPH Distributors (S) Pte., Ltd., 601 Sims Drive, #03/07/21, Singapore 1438; in the PHILIPPINES by Bio-Research, 5 Lippay Street, San Lorenzo Village, Makati Rizal; in SOUTH AFRICA by Multipet Pty. Ltd., 30 Turners Avenue, Durban 4001. Published by T.F.H. Publications, Inc. Manufactured in the United States of America by T.F.H. Publications, Inc.

CONTENTS

Man playing a hammered dulcimer, an instrument similar to the clavichord, but without a keyboard. The strings are struck from above with hand-held mallets. This instrument enjoyed a brief period of great popularity at the opening of the 18th century due to the virtuosity of one Pantaleon Hebenstreit.

1. BACK TO PYTHAGORAS

"The sum of the squares of the legs of a right triangle is equal to the square of the hypotenuse." Does it ring a bell? Of course, you might say—Pythagoras.

But why recall the venerable mathematician in a book on music? To answer this question, let us travel 2,500 years back in time to the coast of the Aegean Sea. We shall find ourselves in ancient Greece, in a period that would be named the "May of Life" and the "Spring of Mankind" centuries later.

That was the wonderful land of the Hellenes. They worshipped beauty, and life without art was meaningless to them. "He who has never seen the statue of Zeus Olympius sculpted by the great Phideas cannot be happy in life," they said.

An ancient Greek philosopher proclaimed: "Music is a powerful force. It can make a human being love or hate, forgive or kill."

MUSIC. We are accustomed to this word and often use it without suspecting that it was born in Hellas, or ancient Greece, over twenty-five centuries ago, just as were the words melody, rhythm, and gamut.

In ancient Greek mythology the Muses, nine daughters of Mnemosyne (Memory) and Zeus, presided over the arts and sciences. Terpsichore was the Muse of dancing and choral song, Erato the Muse of love and love poetry, Euterpe the Muse of lyric song and music. The word music itself derives from the Muses. The mythical goddesses gave birth to another word in common use today as well: museum. In Hellas, museums or mouseions were temples of the Muses. This word has retained its original meaning to this day. Museums are indeed veritable temples, in which people admire the beauty of art.

The leader of the Muses was the Olympian god Apollo, therefore called Apollo Musagete. Ancient Greek sculptors often depicted Apollo with a kithara, or large lyre, in his hands. According to mythology, Apollo had been so entranced with the lyre that he acquired it from its inventor, Hermes, and made it his own.

Orpheus, son of Calliope, the Muse of eloquence and epic poetry, personified the magic power of music. His singing to the lyre was so enchanting that it could keep beasts, rocks and trees spellbound. As soon as they heard his song, ferocious wild animals became as docile as lambs, formidable granite boulders retreated before him, and forests bowed their branches to him in silent admiration. When his beloved bride Euridice died, bitten by a serpent, Orpheus undertook a voyage attempted by no other mortal: he descended to the underground kingdom of the dead, Hades, and, with his music, lulled to sleep the three-headed watchdog Cerberus, who guarded the portals of the nether world, moved the three Fates to tears, and made the boatman of the river Styx, Charon, carry him across in the ferry in which no living human had ever before set foot. So powerful was the Orphic song that Persephone, Queen of the infernal regions, was full of admiration, and the proud ruler Pluto himself agreed to let Orpheus lead his Euridice back to the realm of the living. That Orpheus lost his bride for the second time before regaining the light of day does not diminish the near omnipotence of his music.

The myth of Orpheus was very popular in ancient Greece, because the Hellenes loved music as much as the other arts. Their dances, gymnastic contests, and pantomime were invariably accompanied by music. Hellenic poets were often depicted, like Apollo, with lyre or kithara in hand. When, in the Renaissance, an attempt was made to recapture the art of ancient Greek declamation, a simple accompaniment by plucked instruments of the lute family was chosen as most closely approximating the sound of the ancient bard singing to his lyre. Any satirical drama or tragedy in the ancient Greek theatre was performed to the accompaniment of singing and music.

Although the ancient Greeks had a number of musical instruments at their disposal, including the double pipe or aulos, (activated by reeds somewhat like those of the bagpipe), pan-pipes, and various percussion instruments, the lyre and kithara were the instruments most often associated with art music. Both the lyre and the kithara were held more or less upright, and had strings plucked with the fingers or by a thin plate of some hard material called a plectrum. The lyre, according to Homer's Hymn to Mercury, was invented by Hermes (Mercury) who stretched sheep gut strings supported by an antelope horn frame across a soundbox or resonator made of a tortoise shell. The descendants of this simple instrument are known as bowl lyres to distinguish them from kithara-type instruments or box lyres, whose resonators, while still lying in the same plane as the strings and their supporting yoke, are more box-like in shape.

The two related instruments, lyre and kithara, must have enjoyed in their time much of the popularity given the piano in our own era. Singing, pantomime, and playing musical instruments were regular subjects in educating young people. Contests in the art of musical performance formed part of the Olympic and Pythian games, and monuments to celebrated musicians were erected in city squares.

Music, however, was not regarded only as an art of entertainment or a part of ceremony. The ancient Greek philosophers were confident that all things in the universe were in perfect harmony and that direct relationships existed between music and astronomy, mu-

Dulcimer strings could be plucked directly with the fingers, or by means of hand-held quills or plectra.

The dulcimer or psaltery exhibits the tone-producing parts common to all pianos, harpsichords, and clavichords: strings mounted on bridges and stretched across a soundboard.

sic and philosophy, music and mathematics. Pythagoras, the author of the famous theorum, was one of the many thinkers from ancient times through the seventeenth century who studied the relationships between music, mathematics, and astronomy. According to the views of Pythagoras and his followers, the universe and its individual planets were a system of mathematical relationships similar to those on which music is based, a "music of the spheres." Pythagoras maintained that the universe was a harmony of relationships between numbers corresponding to the intervals between the different degrees of the musical scale. The great scientist also took a keen interest in questions pertaining to musical modes and intervals. His research into the properties of intervals led him to the discovery that whole number ratios may be used to express the octave (2:1), the 5th (3:2), the 4th (4:3), and the major 2nd (9:8). Popular legend has it that this theory of intervals was developed as Pythagoras heard the sounds produced by hammers striking anvils of various sizes, but he may also have made use of the monochord, a single-stringed musical instrument consisting of a long hollow wooden resonating box with a string stretched over its upper surface. Near each end of the string was a bridge, or upright wooden piece which defined the portion of the string that would be set into vibration when the string was struck with a little hammer or plucked. One of these bridges could be moved to different points, allowing measurement of the vibrating length of the string (and thus of the corresponding pitches produced) according to a graduated scale inscribed on the upper part of the resonating box. By shifting the moveable bridge to different points, Pythagoras was able to achieve an accuracy in his measurements of different intervals which had hitherto escaped theoreticians.

Even if the great Greek mathematician and his followers were mistaken in their belief that music and the universe were governed by the same mathematical laws, some of their discoveries laid the groundwork for later developments of western musical theory. As far as the monochord is concerned, it was one of the first small steps towards the invention of the piano.

2. THE SILVER-VOICED CLAVICHORD

Relatives of many of the musical instruments used by the ancient Greeks may still be found in less technologically advanced societies even today. Some, undergoing considerable refinement of design, may now be seen as ancestors of the instruments in use in contemporary western music: these include various flutes, drums, and, to some extent, the monochord. The lyre and kithara, however, have no direct descendants save the harp, which differs from them substantially in the relative alignments of its strings and resonator.

The monochord is closely related to two other instruments, the dulcimer and the psaltery, which have for centuries occupied important places in folk music of widely diverse cultures. In these instruments, the simple wooden resonator box of the monochord, easy to make and convenient to handle, carries not one but many strings, stretched across a series of bridges. Dulcimers, psalteries and other varieties of the monochord were for centuries invariable assistants of the song teachers and loyal companions of vagrant musicians, actors, buffoons, and jesters. (Today, the dulcimer still is popular as a folk instrument, and the autoharp, a semi-mechanized dulcimer designed to facilitate the playing of strummed chords for accompaniment, is often used in schools.) Travelling from town to town and from village to village, these itinerant entertainers performed in squares and castles before peasants and kings, singing satirical ditties about greedy aristocrats and cruel feudal knights and moving love songs in honor of revered ladies, often to the accompaniment of a psaltery or dulcimer. The thirty or more strings of some of the larger medieval psalteries must have challenged even the skilled musician, who had to exercise great care in order to move cleanly amidst the web of strings.

Medieval musicians and instrument builders searched with determination to build more sophisticated models. By the early Middle Ages, the organ, already known in ancient times, was a familiar instrument. The organ, essentially a series of wind-blown pipes activated singly or in combination by levers or keys, provided a model for the attachment of a keyboard to the descendants of the monochord.

The first keyboard-activated instruments in which the tone was produced by the vibration of strings was probably the organistrum, a medieval hurdy-gurdy first described in the 10th century by Odo of Cluny, and depicted in numerous medieval sculptures. This hurdy-gurdy was in no way like the barrel organ of similar name associated with monkeys and organ grinders, but was rather a long or pear-shaped resonating box equipped with several strings set into vibration by the action of a rosined wheel which rotated against them. In this fashion, it has some remote relationship to the many scattered folk instruments with one bowed string stretched across a box resembling that of the psaltery, of which the Russian gusli is but one example. Odo's instructions for building an organistrum include references to the movable bridge of the monochord as a guide for placement of the key rods which press against the non-drone string of the instrument, eliciting from it different pitches. Folk descendants of the organistrum, for the most part rather smaller in size, were quite popular in western Europe at least through the time of the French Revolution.

From the 14th century, we have several references to an instrument with the unlikely name of eschaqueil (or eschaquier) d'Angleterre, or "English chessboard," also known as

Young woman playing a clavichord (painting attributed to Jan van Hemessen, Flemish, 1500-66).

Anonymous German clavichord, 18th century (Smithsonian Institution). The clavichord's strings are struck with brass tangents inserted into the ends of the keys. This simple mechanism, allowing for dynamic variation, is the true predecessor of the modern piano action.

the "chekker." The exact form of this instrument remains a mystery, despite many studies, but it appears to have been some kind of keyboard-activated dulcimer: one theory suggests that the alternation of black and white key buttons may have resembled the squares of a chessboard, another, now less popular, claims that like the game of chess, the chekker may have had its origins in the Orient. By about 1440, Henri Arnault de Zwolle was able to write a treatise giving four different ways a string-activating mechanism could be applied to a keyboard.

The simplest method of exciting a string into vibration from a keyboard is that embodied in the clavichord. ("Clavichord" derives from the Latin word for "key" and the Greek word for "string.") The history of the clavichord is shrouded in etymological confusion, as, at times, instruments with more than one string are called variously "monochords" and "polychords," but it now appears that the first clavichords date from the end of the 14th century. The clavichord action is nothing more than a key lever mounted at one end with a small upright piece of brass called the tangent. When the key is depressed from the opposite end, the tangent strikes the string, causing it to vibrate, and, at the same time, determining the vibrating length of the string by acting like the movable bridge of the monochord. The strings of the oldest type of clavichord were all of the same length and diameter, and would consequently have all produced the same pitch were it not for the fact that they were struck at different points by the tangents. Because the tangent determined the speaking length of the string, several keys, each with its own tangent, could activate the same string, striking it at different places to produce different pitches. Clavichord makers found this a convenient way to reduce the number of strings necessary in an instrument, thereby reducing the tension on the frame and allowing for a lighter overall construction. Tuning, too, was easier in these instruments, known as "fretted" clavichords to distinguish them from "unfretted" instruments in which the number of strings equalled the number of keys, with each tangent striking its own string. Unfretted clavichords, though more time-consuming to tune than fretted instruments, had the advantage that any desired combination of notes could be struck at the same time: on fretted instruments, one could not simultaneously use the keys whose tangents hit one and the same string.

The most obvious feature of a clavichord, however, be it fretted or unfretted, is its general softness. Because the tangent at once both imparts energy to the string and serves to divide that same string into a vibrating section and a non-vibrating section, the amount of energy actually transferred to the string is quite small, as the string is naturally very stiff near any nodal point such as that set up by the tangent. (By plucking a violin, guitar, or piano string both near its bridge, and somewhat towards its center, the reader can readily test the veracity of this assertion.) To make the instrument somewhat louder, clavichord makers frequently used two, or even three, strings in place of a single string, but the clavichord's voice remained delicate. Despite its quietness, which precludes its use as an accompanying instrument, the clavichord is capable of a graduated dynamic range, ranging from almost inaudible to only moderately soft. In a properly intimate setting, however, this expressivity can seem to span the entire spectrum of dynamics from the most ethereal pianissimo to the boldest fortissimo. Furthermore, since the tangent remained in contact with the string as long as the key was depressed, a vibrato, or small fluctuation in pitch, could be produced by varying the amount of pressure on the key, thereby slightly changing the tension of the string. Because of its capacity for this so-called Bebung, unique among keyboard instruments, and its infinitely variable dynamic range, the shortcomings of the clavichord could easily be overlooked, and musicians and poets could describe its merits with the most superlative epithets, lavishing praises upon its "plaintive," "comforting," "sweet," and "silvery" sounds. It was called "a consolation in grief and a friend in joy." From its origins until the end of the 1700s, the clavichord was unexcelled for its expressive and delicate sonority, especially in conveying pensive moods and sorrow. Its relative portability and ease of construction had made it popular during the Renaissance and Baroque periods. Expanded in compass and overall dimensions, it was a favorite of musicians like C.P.E. Bach during the period between the death of Johann Sebastian Bach and the ascendency of Mozart. From an unassumingly modest size small enough to to be held in the lap, the clavichord evolved into a free-standing, and often elaborately decorated, instrument with a five octave range, while still retaining its remarkably simple mechanism. It was only the advent of the piano that relegated it to temporary oblivion.

Plan view of a German clavichord, made in 1756 by Johann Adolf Hass of Hamburg (Smithsonian Institution), showing splayed key levers typical of fretted clavichords, and floral soundboard decoration.

3. THE HARPSICHORD AND ITS LARGE FAMILY

Like that of the clavichord, the early history of the harpsichord is not fully known. Its names in non-English speaking countries—cembalo in Italy, clavicimbalo or simply cembalo in Germany, and clavecin in France—all betray something of its origin. Cimbal, cimbalom, cymbali, and cymbalki are Austrian, Hungarian, Russian, and Polish words for various kinds of dulcimers: the Latin clavis designates "key" here as it did in the case of the clavichord. As is evident from Arnault de Zwolle's treatise, from at least the 15th century, instrument makers were striving to produce keyboard instruments that sounded louder than the clavichord. They had no doubt noticed that performers could elicit fairly loud sounds from dulcimers or psalteries by plucking the strings somewhere near their centers. Attaching a keyboard with a plucking mechanism to such an instrument was rather more complicated than building a clavichord, but by the middle decades of the 15th century, the problems were, in principle, overcome.

The new instrument differed from the somewhat older clavichord in several ways. First, because the strings were plucked with a quill rather than struck with a tangent which determined their speaking length, each string had to be of a different length, sounding a different pitch. For practical purposes, the wing shape familiar today as that of the grand piano, with the short treble strings at the right side of the keyboard, and the longer bass strings running out as much as several yards from the left-most keys, was evolved. In contrast to the clavichord, where the string band ran across the length of the keys, in the harpsichord, the strings continued out, as it were, from the lines set out by the key levers. As in the earlier instrument, the strings of the harpsichord were fixed at one end by a loop over a pin sunk in a wooden framing member, and at the other by a movable tuning pin by which their tension could be regulated, but rather than passing over only one bridge, harpsichord strings were required to touch two bridges, one mounted on the soundboard, the other on the pinblock, which effectively determined their speaking length.

The mechanism of sound elicitation used in the harpsichord is rather more elaborate than the simple tangent design of the clavichord. Sitting atop the far end of each key lever are one or more jacks, small upright pieces of wood which glide up and down in wooden (or wood-and-leather) guides. Near the top of each jack is a movable wooden tongue which pivots on a pin. The tongue is provided with a small hole for a quill or leather plectrum which projects at right angles to the body of the jack, and which sits, when the key is not depressed, just below the string it serves. When the player depresses a key, the jack at its

Italian harpsichord by Nicolaus DeQuoco, 1694 (Smithsonian Institution). Use of materials varied from place to place: this instrument shows the boxwood naturals and ebony-covered sharps commonly used on Italian keyboards.

opposite end is thrown up in the air, causing the plectrum to pluck the string as it passes during its ascent. When the key is released, the jack falls back down with gravity, and the tongue swivels back to allow the plectrum to pass by the string without replucking. When the jack comes to rest, a cloth strip called the damper protruding from its top effectively stops the string from vibrating.

The volume of the harpsichord was indeed louder than that of its smaller-voiced cousin, but, due to the size and stiffness of the plectra (usually made from the quill of crow, turkey, raven, or condor feathers), the player had no control over the volume of any particular. string. As the author of one treatise put it, a harpsichord had to be "uniformly feathered" to give listening pleasure. The fragile nature of the plectrum material required frequent maintenance, but it was precisely this delicate "plumage" of the harpsichord that accounted in large measure for its beautiful sound effects. To achieve dynamic contrasts, makers equipped their instruments with several sets of strings, each activated by its own set of jacks (in special instances, two sets, or registers, of jacks could pluck the same string at different points). With only one set of strings engaged, a harpsichord was at its softest. Adding a second set made it rather louder, and also changed its tone color. A third set, often tuned an octave higher than the first two, gave yet a different character and quantity of sound. Larger instruments had two keyboards, and, in Germany, a third keyboard and additional sets of strings were not unknown. The most usual disposition for a large 18th-century harpsichord was probably two keyboards or manuals, which could be linked together by a mechanical coupler (so that both could be played from the lower) controlling two strings at regular ("eight-foot" or 8') pitch, and one set an octave higher ("four-foot" or 4' pitch). Some builders added an extra set of jacks which plucked the strings very close to the pinblock bridge, or nut, producing the nasal sound which characterizes this so-called "nazard" or "lute" stop. Another coloristic device often fitted to harpsichords was the buff stop, in which a series of pieces of very soft leather was brought into contact with the strings near the nut, partially damping the sound immediately upon the string being plucked.

As is the case with many musical instruments, harpsichords (and, to a somewhat lesser extent, clavichords) can be distinguished along lines of national origin. Italian instruments

This double-manual harpsichord made by Johannes Daniel Dulcken in Antwerp in 1745 (Smithsonian Institution) has four registers, each activated by its own row of jacks. These registers can be played singly or together in various combinations.

are among the earliest now extant. They are distinguished throughout three centuries of manufacture (through the last part of the 1700s) by their elegant lines and light cypress construction. Flemish harpsichords, rather heavier in design, were brought to perfection in the 17th century by the Ruckers family, working under guidelines established through traditional guilds. French makers followed and expanded upon Flemish models during the later 17th century and well into the 18th. English and German makers each pursued their own designs. Each school of building produced instruments which were distinctive not only for their musical sounds, but for their decorative qualities as well. In addition to the familiar wing shape, upright harpsichords or clavicytheria, rectangular harpsichords or virginals, and roughly triangular models called spinets were produced.

Despite the care lavished on its construction, however, no harpsichord was able to overcome one inherent musical characteristic, one that was to be seen as a critical flaw as the piano gained ascendency at the end of the 18th century: the strength of pressure exerted on a key had almost no effect on the intensity or volume of the sound produced. The sounds produced by the action of the quill (or, in exceptional cases, leather) plectra were fairly loud but not as flexible and pliant as the gentle and expressive tones of the clavichord, with its metal tangents. But were the clavichord and the harpsichord rivals or equal partners? Which of them was more important and enjoyed primacy?

"Whoever wants to hear delicacy in playing and purity in embellishments should listen to the exquisite magic sounds of the clavichord, because the sounds of the large clavicembalo have a restless and noisy breath which makes a good rendition impossible." So spoke one 17th-century proponent of the softer instrument. Another experienced musician of the period gave this advice to his pupil: "At first you should learn to play the clavichord, because as soon as you acquire the knack of it, you will find it easier to play the organ, the clavicembalo, the virginal, and other keyboard instruments." Other ardent admirers of the clavichord were more categorical in comparing the two instruments: "He who prefers the cembalo to the clavichord has no heart and is a poor musician."

The harpsichord, however, had no less enthusiastic supporters. They praised its universality, which gave it obvious advantages over the clavichord, and said: "Just as the organ incorporates all the wind instruments, the harpsichord has assembled all the strings within itself: the viol, the harp, and the lute." The harpsichord had yet another merit: it was a far better instrument for developing finger strength. Carl Philipp Emanuel Bach, one of Johann Sebastian's most gifted sons, remarked that "if one plays only the clavichord one may lose forever one's finger strength." It was precisely this C.P.E. Bach, who was not only an outstanding composer but also a remarkable performer, who wisely reconciled the contrary points of view regarding the harpsichord and the clavichord.

Anonymous Italian harpsichord, 1693 (Smithsonian Institution). Like most Italian harpsichords, the simple cypress case of the instrument itself was designed to fit in a more elaborately decorated protective outer case.

Every good keyboard player should have a good harpsichord and a good clavichord to be able to play various types of music on them alternately. He who plays the clavichord well enough will be able to play the harpsichord, but not the other way around. Thus, one who wants to learn to play well should use the clavichord, and one who wants to develop his finger strength should use the harpsichord. A musician accustomed to playing the clavichord will encounter quite a few difficulties in playing the harpsichord. He will find it hard to play clavier music to the accompaniment of other instruments. This music has to be played on the harpsichord, because the sound of the clavichord is too faint. It is known that what is worked out with difficulty cannot make a good impression on the listener. In playing the clavichord, one is wont to caress the keys. As a result, in playing the harpsichord some details may occasionally be missed, because the pressure on the keys is insufficient. On the other hand, if a keyboardist constantly plays only on the harpsichord, he will become accustomed to playing all music in identical colors.

Virginal by Andreas Ruckers, Antwerp, 1620 (Smithsonian Institution). Harpsichords in this shape are known as virginals. This small example, tuned a fourth above standard pitch, shows the elaborate block-printed paper decoration typically employed by Flemish harpsichord makers.

Plan view of the Ruckers virginal, showing floral motifs surrounding the gilded soundboard rose, which displays the maker's initials and device, David playing his harp. Here the keyboard coverings are of bone and ebony.

A plan view of a Steinway and Sons square piano, New York, 1877-78 (Smithsonian Institution). The square piano continued to be of real musical interest during the last quarter of the 19th century only in the United States.

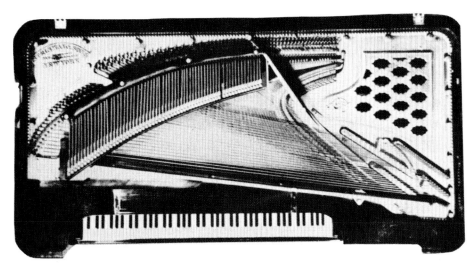

Action model of a 17th-century Italian harpsichord. The quill plectrum in the jack on the upper left is in the process of plucking the high-lighted string.

In this way, C.P.E. Bach accurately discriminated between the acoustic potentials and distinctions of technique proper to each instrument, and defined their relative merits and demerits. Keyboard artists of the 17th and 18th centuries, when the harpsichord and clavichord enjoyed their greatest primacy, were able to use the two instruments to their best advantage, and it is certain that their artistry, both as executants and as composers, was no less than that of the greatest pianist/composers of the 19th and 20th centuries, just as we consider Leonardo the equal of Picasso, though the two men worked in entirely different styles. Let us now meet some of these keyboard giants from the time before the advent of the piano.

KARL PHILIPP EMANUEL
BACH.

Carl Philipp Emanuel Bach (1714–1788). Etching by J. Krüger.

WILH: FRIEDEMAÑ BACH

ehemahliger Musikdirect u Organist
zu Halle

Geb: in Weimar 1710 Gestorben zu Berlin 1784

Wilhelm Friedemann Bach (1710–1784). Etching by C. Schwenterley.

Johann Christian Bach (1735–1782). Painting by T. Gainsborough.

Johann Sebastian Bach, a modern caricature.

IV. THE WIZARDS OF MUSIC

In the autumn of 1717 the residents of the German town of Dresden learned exciting news that immediately became the talk of the town. The famous French harpsichordist, organist, and composer Louis Marchand had arrived in Dresden. So great was his virtuosity that Parisian music lovers had followed him from church to church in the French capital, raptly listening to his organ improvisations. He now appeared in Dresden, ready to challenge the finest German keyboardist to a musical duel.

At that time, musical tournaments testing the improvising skills of their participants were not uncommon. A contestant was offered a theme–a short musical passage or the melody of a popular song or aria–on which he was to compose his own work immediately, right in front of the eyes (and ears) of his audience. The improvisation was expected to display the player's skill both in composition and performance. Such contests sometimes lasted as long as several hours, to the delight and admiration of the listeners.

Marchand, a favorite of Louis XIV of France, had a widespread reputation, and had toured extensively in Germany in 1713. Perhaps because of his favorable reception at that time, no German aspirant came forward to meet his challenge at first, but finally his call was answered. A 32-year-old Kapellmeister from the ducal court of Weimar came to Dresden to cross musical swords with the 47-year-old Frenchman.

The contest so eagerly awaited by all, however, never took place. According to the German chroniclers of the event, as soon as he learned his opponent's name, Marchand, fearing defeat, fled Dresden, nevermore to show his face there. French writers of the 18th century were more kind, claiming that Marchand's return to Paris shortly after the Dresden debacle was due to homesickness. Whatever the cause, Marchand might well have had reason to tremble, for Johann Sebastian Bach, already famous in 1717, is revered today as one of the greatest musicians who ever lived.

Numerous surviving documentary testimonies from his contemporaries show admiration for Bach's superlative playing. The following is typical: Herr Johann Sebastian Bach, Kapellmeister at the court of Prince Leopold of Anhalt-Cothen, and cantor of St. Thomas's Church in Leipzig, who arrived here from Leipzig a few days ago, played the organ at the Church of St. Sophia before an audience of courtiers, musicians, and virtuosos so wonderfully that all were beside themselves with delight. A poet who was among the listeners wrote this inspired verse: The gurgle of a stream charms our ear, This music of the earth to our hearts is dear, But what we hear from the human stream [Bach is German for "stream"] By far excells our most blissful dream. In days of yore the lyre of Orpheus in Greece With magic harmony enchanted rocks and beasts, But when our Bach works wonders at the organ No human can escape his magic charm. While most of his contemporaries felt similarly, others found fault with his compositions, which they characterized as "long and boring." Many of Bach's finest works were but infrequently performed during his lifetime, and only a small portion of his music was published before his death. Still, his keyboard music is among the finest ever written, and much of what Bach wrote for the harpsichord or clavichord forms today the very foundation of the piano literature.

A great debate still rages between partisans of the piano, on the one hand, and defenders of the harpsichord on the other, with one side arguing that "if Bach had known the piano, he certainly would have written for it," while the other wishes to keep both feet

St. Thomas Church and School in Leipzig as it looked in 1723 in a drawing by J. G. Krüger.

firmly planted on what is historically possible, rather than indulging in unprovable speculation. The controversy is fueled by the fact that Bach was the champion of several "new" instruments, among them the Lautenwerk, or "lute harpsichord," whose sounds were so much like those of the lute, one of the most favored instruments of the period, that even professional musicians were unable to say with certainty whether they came from a lute or a harpsichord. Bach did in fact play on several early pianos, and was reportedly unimpressed by them. He did, however, make a substantial contribution to our modern method of tuning pianos through an important series of compositions which deserves some technical explanation.

Since before the advent of the harpsichord, the musical scale had been divided into twelve half steps, or semi-tones. The modern piano keyboard, with its seven white and five black keys per octave, reflects this division, and indeed the distinction is discernible in almost all earlier keyboards as well, though their keys may be covered with different materials than the white and black plastic (ersatz ivory and ebony) so frequently encountered today. Each of these twelve keys could serve as the base for either a major or a minor tonality, making twenty-four theoretically available tonalities, or "keys," which a composer might employ. In fact, however, due to the systems of tuning employed until Bach's time (and even, in many cases, well beyond), only those keys with a relatively small number of sharps and flats sounded well in tune on keyboard instruments. When compositions modulated into keys with many sharps or flats, the tuning system or temperament in use made them

The most popular "official" portrait of J. S. Bach.

sound unbearably false or out of tune. Therefore, composers had for centuries satisfied themselves with using only a bit more than half of the theoretically available tonalities, which, in the temperaments available to them, were of an unparalleled purity.

Theoreticians, among them one Andreas Werkmeister of Halberstadt, who was also an organ builder, had for some time before Bach discussed the possibilities of other tuning systems in which the half steps or semi-tones could be made more equal in size, allowing utilization of some of the tonalities which had till then been avoided, while at the same time not seriously compromising the purity enjoyed by the "good" tonalities. Werkmeister's inquiries, however, remained unconfirmed theory until the appearance of a volume of music whose author inscribed it title page: THE WELL-TEMPERED CLAVIER or Preludes and Fugues through all the tones and semi-tones both as regards the tertia major or Ut Re Mi and as concerns the tertia minor or Re Mi Fa. For the Use and Profit of the Musical Youth

Desirous of Learning as well as for the Pastime of those Already Skilled in this Study drawn up and written by Johann Sebastian Bach p.t. Kapellmeister to His Serene Highness the Prince of Anhalt-Cothen, etc. and Director of His Chamber Music Anno 1722. Thus, for the first time in the history of keyboard (clavier) instruments, musicians were given proof of the possibilities afforded by all 24 tonalities. Twenty-two years later, six years before his death, Bach completed a second set of 24 preludes and fugues. Taken together, the "forty-eight," as these works are known, have a significance for the history of keyboard music (and, by extension, for the art of pianism) so great as to defy description in words. As a testament to Bach's instructional genius, they excel even the two- and three-part Inventions, and must have formed part of the musical diet both of Bach's own children and of his other pupils.

Because of the reverence accorded to Bach's keyboard music, it is all too easy to neglect the fact that, during his lifetime, other giants of the keyboard were also active, many of them outside of Germany. France, for example, could boast numerous examples of excellent performers, gifted composers, and skilled instrument makers during the late 17th and early 18th centuries. "French musicians play the harpsichord with a delicacy unexcelled anywhere," wrote one eyewitness. Another seconded this opinion: "Their instruments are so advanced that it is hard to make improvements in their design." Dozens of first-rate harpsichordists worked at the courts of Louis XIV and Louis XV, and many aristocrats of the time were accomplished keyboard players, as the market for printed clavecin music proves.

A sample of Johann Sebastian Bach's handwriting.

Let us imagine ourselves at a concert of harpsichord music in a French aristocratic salon of the early 18th century. Such concerts were favorite pastimes of the nobility. The brilliance of costume, the elegance of the furniture, and the wealth of detail in the room's appointments are matched by the workmanship exhibited in the harpsichord, which is the focus of attention. The works selected for performance are drawn from suites, or orders, consisting of dance movements and character pieces, or miniature musical portraits, refined and stylized as everything else in the milieu of the French aristocracy.

With such a charming but superficial picture in our mind's eye, it is all too easy to imagine that the composers of clavecin music, the clavecinistes, were content to dabble in the aurally pleasant without plumbing the depths of human emotion with their works. While it is true that their output contains numerous "pictures in music" of such inconsequential things as cuckoos, bees, and butterflies, the tonal portraits painted by Jean-Philippe Rameau or Francois Couperin allow us insightful glimpses of the strong personalities they portray. Couperin, called "le Grand" by his contemporaries to distinguish him from other talented members of his family, wrote: "Composing my pieces, I always had in mind a definite theme suggested by various circumstances. Therefore, their titles correspond to the ideas that guided me in their composition. I would call them portraits of their own kind. . ."

Indeed, Couperin created a complete gallery of portraits in music. Some of his works depict the images of living people surrounding him, among them his family, his colleagues,

Francois Couperin

Francois Couperin Compositeur Organiste de la Chapelle du Roy.

29

and his friends. Others, devoted to general traits of the human character and different moods rather than to concrete images, are no less interesting. With the sounds of the harpsichord, Couperin and his great contemporaries depicted coquetry, diffidence, passion, and gloom. In some of their works, they conjure up scenes of rural life ("The Grape Harvesters," "The Reapers") or sketches of nature ("Reeds," "The Nightingale in Love"); in others they express ethnic characteristics ("The Proud Spaniard") or paint scenes from their own domestic world ("The Knitters"). 18th-century French character pieces, as such openly descriptive works have come to be called, are among the most famous examples of early programme music for keyboard, pieces in which the composer himself gives a hint of specific extra-musical content. Programme music is often easier to understand than more abstract works, since it offers the listener a point of departure before the first note has been sounded. It was not fortuitous that composers of later periods who wrote piano music often provided their works with descriptive titles, such as Schumann's Carnival, Moussorgsky's Pictures at an Exhibition, or Tchaikovsky's The Seasons. While adoption of the character piece as a genre was not wide-spread, serious composers, including Bach, are known to have studied the music of the great clavecinistes far beyond the borders of France, and the influence of Couperin and his compatriots can be seen not only in Bach's French Suites, but in many other works less self-consciously Gallic.

Turning our backs on the north, let us travel to Italy, called the "land of music," birthplace and training ground for many outstanding composers, famous singers, and brilliant instrumentalists. Italy was the homeland of opera, the concerto, the sonata, and other musical genres. The violin, the 'cello, and—getting ahead of our story—the piano were all invented in Italy.

Domenico Scarlatti playing his harpsichord. Scarlatti was basically an operatic composer, but he has gained immortality with his 500 one-movement harpsichord sonatas, his own invention.

Early masters featured piano-like instruments as signs of culture. Thus a lady sitting at a harpsichord would be considered as a cultured lady.

As in the rest of Europe, however, the harpsichord, or cembalo, as it was called here, was a familiar and favorite instrument throughout Italy. The greatest Italian wizard of the keyboard was Domenico Scarlatti. One listener, upon hearing him play, wrote that it seemed as if it were "not just one man but a thousand devils running their fingers over the keyboard."

Like Johann Sebastian Bach and Francois Couperin, Domenico Scarlatti came from a musical family. His father was the celebrated opera composer Alessandro Scarlatti. The life of the young Scarlatti, however, was quite different from those of his northern contemporaries who, plagued by daily cares and petty problems, never left their native countries. Scarlatti, an equally brilliant virtuoso who made triumphant tours of Europe, showed little concern for the fate of his manuscripts, and thus doomed future students of his art to long

An old etching of Domenico Scarlatti.
by C. Schwenterley.

and arduous quests for whatever was left of them. As a young man he had tried his fortune at various musical genres, but soon fixed his attention on the harpsichord sonata, composing over 500 short, one-movement pieces for his chosen instrument in which his inventiveness and fantasy sparkle like myriad gems. The composer himself was very modest in evaluating the artistic merits of his sonatas, and called them simply "cembalo excercises," writing: "Whether you be an amateur or a professional, you should not seek a profound meaning in these works, but simply play them to get a grasp of harpsichord technique. It was not a profit motive or vanity, but a desire to help you that induced me to publish these pieces. Try to be lenient and moderate in your criticism of them, for this will only add to the pleasure you deserve. I wish you good luck."

Scarlatti could hardly have supposed anything like the fortunate lot prepared by destiny for his "cembalo exercises," which would be given a new lease on life by the piano. "Nature has given us ten fingers, and we have an instrument that can provide them with work, so why not use those fingers to best advantage?" he wrote. In his sonatas, the composer revealed the vast technical and artistic potential of the harpsichord, and anticipated many elements of pianistic technique, including the piano's inherent vocalism. Through these works, an instrument long familiar to all acquired a new voice. According to the 18th-century English music historian Charles Burney, Scarlatti borrowed many themes for his sonatas from "the songs of cabmen, mule drivers, and other plain people." Certainly, Scarlatti's melodies are very vivid and easy to remember.

His statement about the need to put all ten fingers to work takes on new interest when we recall that, until the late 18th century, the thumb was very little used in playing passage-work. It was believed that J. S. Bach had pioneered its use as a matter of course. Now we know, however, that Scarlatti had been another leader in the development of this technique. The employment of all ten fingers enabled musicians to apply sophisticated elements of technique unknown before. Significantly, the great Franz Liszt, whose compositions and style of performance effected a veritable revolution in the art of the piano playing, had thoroughly studied the works of Scarlatti.

For all their genius, Bach, Couperin, and Scarlatti, the greatest wizards of the harpsichord, who composed music for it with full abandon and inspiration, could hardly imagine that their favorite instrument would soon be buried in oblivion for nearly a century. For all that, the piano had been invented well within their lifetime.

5. THE BIRTH OF THE PIANO

A grand reception for the most distinguished citizens was in full progress at the Florentine home of Prince Ferdinando di Medici, the eldest son of the Grand Duke of Tuscany. The soirées arranged by Prince Ferdinand, one of the wealthiest aristocrats in Italy, invariably excited curiosity among the people of Florence. The Prince always had something unusual in store to delight his guests. Be it the premiere of a new play by a fashionable playwright or a new work by a famous composer, a meeting with a celebrated artist or sculptor, or a recital by a touring virtuoso.

An enlightened nobleman and a subtle connoisseur of art, Prince Ferdinand himself was quite at home in the art of harpsichord playing. Whether he stayed at his winter residence, Palazzo Pitti, or at his summer retreat at Pratolino, he always had excellent instruments at his disposal. Prince Ferdinand's collection of harpsichords was famous far beyond Italy's borders.

The custodian of his collection Bartolomeo Cristofori, whose lifelong occupation was designing and building harpsichords. This time again he had come up with something new, which the Prince wanted to present as a big surprise to his guests.

...The guests assembled in a spacious hall, exquisitely furnished and decorated, and looked with curiosity at the instrument concealed under its cloth cover.

"Gravicembalo col piano e forte,"* Cristofori announced. Guests were chatting casually, looking at him from time to time. *That's a funny name the Paduan master gave to his brainchild,* someone remarked. Another said: *"There's talk in town about some leathercoated hammers he has fitted into the cembalo instead of the jacks pins. Funny, isn't it?"*

But all fell silent as Cristofori took his seat at the keyboard. The cover removed, and the instrument came to life under his deft fingers . . . Before the last sounds were died down, listeners were already exchanging glances and excited whispered comments.

"Interesting, very interesting. But the ordinary harpsichord sounds better, and then we are used to it."

"There's nothing unusual about this one either. Just take a look at its shape..."

One of the guests summed up the argument: *"It is simply another experiment. Many have tried to invent a better clavier, but they tried in vain. The harpsichord will never be bested."*

The demonstration was over. The guests were invited to a neighboring hall where another entertainment had been prepared for them. The new instrument was promptly forgotten.

Cristofori ruefully closed the lid of the instrument, whose novelty has failed to impress Prince Ferdinand's guests. None of them had realized that it was a radically new type of musical instrument. Cristofori was confident, however, that his "hammer-clavier" had a great future. It would, in time win universal recognition.

*A harpsichord of quiet and loud sounds (Italian).

It was around 1710 when Bartolomeo Cristofori demonstrated his hammer-clavier to his masters' guests. He was at the time the first inventor of the new instrument, the first, indeed, but not the only one among those who had arrived at the idea of building a hammer-clavier. In 1716 the model of a similar instrument was built by the Frenchman Marius. A year later the German musician Gottlieb Schröter, organist at the Hauptkirche in Nordhausen, also assembled a hammer-clavier independently of Cristofori and Marius.

It would seem that the remarkable ability of the new instrument to change dynamics should have immediately induced musicians to prefer it to the harpsichord. The latter, however, was stubbornly holding its ground. The mechanism of the early pianos was imperfect, and their tone, though it could be varied in intensity, was sharp and dry.

First comments on the new instrument were too skeptical to gladden musicians. *"The pianoforte is not as sonorous as the harpsichord,"* an acknowledged authority on music said, for instance, in the early 18th century. *"This is a chamber instrument, and hence it is no good for playing loud music."*

Another authority, who was a native of France, seconded him: *"The trebles of the piano are charming, it is true, but the basses are too harsh and dull and seem devoid of succulence to our French ears."*

The great Johann Sebastian Bach, once he had become familiar with first specimens of the piano, also pointed out their essential flaws. In the high register, as he concluded, their tone was too weak, and they were much too hard to play.

Indeed, as compared with the pliancy of the harpsichord the pressure on the piano keys demanded greater effort. Many musicians believed that the need to overcome this additional resistance made it impossible to achieve the ease and fluency of the harpsichord.

"This upstart will never defeat the majestic harpsichord" was the final verdict many pronounced on the newly-born "hammer-clavier", or the pianoforte, as it was sometimes called. Their sentence, however, was repealed by further developments.

Johann Sebastian Bach was not destined to write music for the piano. His youngest son Johann Christian Bach, however, who was a well-known composer and an excellent keyboard player, immediately appreciated the advantages of the new instrument. He was one of the first musicians to give a solo piano recital in public. Before long he published a collection of his sonatas whose subtitle read: **"For Piano forte".**

In the last quarter of the 18th century, many leading instrument makers of Europe began to build pianos. The public attitude to the new instrument quickly changed in its favor. Now the harpsichord was under attack. It was found that its "dull and sharp tone" was a handicap to the performance of "melodious passages." The harpsichord was suffering defeat as a solo instrument. After some two dozen years eyewitnesses of that "great musical revolution" testified that the "harpsichord has survived only in orchestras and one only has to wonder why it is still in use: its tone is so sharp and shrill that it offends the ear." Thus, the harpsichord was condemned to death as an orchestral instrument as well.

The further destiny of the harpsicord was very unfortunate. Few harpsicords made any longer actually faced the danger of total extermination. Since the demand for pianos was rising so rapidly that factories and workshops were unable to keep up with it and supply all clients with new instruments on time, old claviers were taken apart and used to make pianos. As a result, harpsichords became almost extinct. They were buried in oblivion for almost a century.

The late 18th century was the watershed between the reign of the harpsichord and that of the piano.

Plan view of a large French double-manual harpsichord by Jean Mari DeDeBan, Paris, 1770 (Smithsonian Institution). Like their Flemish predecessors, 18th-century French makers used painted floral designs on their soundboards, but covered their keyboards with ebony and ivory.

6. THE MUSICAL CAPITAL OF THE WORLD

In the latter half of the 18th century and in the early 19th there was much dispute as to which was the most important city of Europe. Geographers named one city, historians another, and men of letters still another. Only musicians and lovers of piano music were in full agreement on this point. For them the capital of Europe and the musical world as a whole was the city of Vienna.

The destiny of the piano had been well received at last and was now a much favored instrument in almost every corner of Europe. Public piano performances were common in most large cities, and the art of pianism became a regular subject of musical instruction.

The DeDeBan's two keyboards. The upper keyboard may be coupled to the lower by shoving it towards the nameboard of the instrument, allowing all jacks to be activated from the lower keyboard. The knee levers for engaging registers, visible below the apron stand, are an unusual feature of this late French instrument.

The rose of the DeDeBan.

However, we need only to recall the most outstanding composers of that period. They wrote music for the piano and thus revolutionized the art of musical performance to visualize in our mind's eye the city of Vienna with its majestic palaces and cathedrals, beautiful streets and squares.

Over the ensuing 200 years since then the city has changed beyond recognition. The banks of the Danube are clad in granite. Narrow cobbled lanes with squat 17th and 18th century houses have survived in some quarters to date, and a tourist sightseeing in the city is invariably advised to visit them and see the historic places where famous musicians of the past lived and worked.

Let us also make a short tour of Vienna's "musical sights."

We shall start out, of course, from one of the city's central squares, the site of the famous St. Stephen Cathedral whose enormous steeple tower soars high into the sky. It was here, in the chapel of Her Majesty Queen Maria Theresa that Franz Joseph Haydn began his musical career at the age of seven.

While he was a soloist of the chapel (choirboys lived in a little house near the cathedral) Haydn was learning to play the violin and the clavier. However, the life of a chorister of the royal chapel, in which he stayed for ten years, was full of hardship and strain. Frequent rehearsals and church service left almost no time for serious training in keyboard technique. In fact, Haydn never became a virtuoso.

The guide leading our sightseeing party through Vienna will probably make the next stop at the Kohlmarkt, where the seventeen-year-old Haydn, expelled from the chapel, settled in the attic of a six-storyed building. His dwelling was squalid and cramped and swept by freezing winds through the cracks in the walls in winter, but the young man never lost heart or lapsed into melancholy. He had a loyal companion with him. That was a small worm-eaten clavichord he would later affectionately refer to as "my old friend."

Once he came home with some sheet music of Philipp Emanuel Bach's clavier sonatas he had just bought at a music shop and played them on his clavichord. He was amazed by their beauty and novelty. At that time he could hardly imagine that his own works in this genre would win far greater popularity than P.E. Bach's sonatas had ever enjoyed and that he would be named the founding father of the symphony, quartet and trio, and one of the pioneers of the genre of piano sonata.

Haydn composed his first sonatas in a period of gradual transition from the old types of clavier--the harpsichord and the clavichord--to the piano. He was one of the pioneering composers who brought out the remarkable potentialities of the new instrument. A brilliant composer of chamber and symphonic music, he realized with perspicacity that with its wide variety of timbres, the piano can sound like a chamber ensemble and even like a full-sized orchestra. Listening to his sonatas, one seems to hear the strings of an orchestra, or a violin solo over the background of the orchestral accompaniment, or the playing of a complete orchestra.

The great Austrian composer also liked to improvise and to compose music at the piano. Indeed, it was in the beauty of melody that Haydn saw the value of musical compositions.

"The charm of music lies in its melody," he used to say, *"and it is hard to invent a melody; the mechanical element in music can be learned through persistence and study, but it takes genius to invent a beautiful melody, and this melody needs no further embellishments to be loved..."*

Haydn's works, wonderfully melodious and cheerful, pervaded with humor and subtle lyricism, are admired for their inimitable beauty in our day, too.

Viennese guides usually round off their stories of Haydn with these words: *"Haydn inspired the art of two other composers of genius who lived in Vienna: Mozart and Beethoven."*

As tourists stop in front of the Opera House, a guide says: *"Vienna owes apologies to Mozart. Neither his opera 'Abduction from the Seraglio' nor even 'Don Giovanni' greatly impressed the fastidious Viennese audiences at first. Their recognition came at a much later date..."*

Wolfgang Amadeus Mozart first came to Vienna as a boy. He was brought here from Salzburg by his father, who was eager to display at the imperial court the extraordinary musical talent of his child prodigy. The playing of the young genius delighted whoever heard him, including the Emperor himself. At a court concert the six-year-old Wolfgang demonstrated his brilliant command of the piano, playing at sight, improvising at length on a theme chosen by listeners at random, and performing his own compositions.

It was in Vienna that Mozart composed his first opera.

Mozart's first steps and successes in music were linked with the piano. He began composing when he was not yet five years of age. His brilliant musicality, extraordinary pianistic skill, phenomenal for his young age, and understanding of the rich possibilities of the piano were not wasted; Mozart became one of the best performing musicians of his time. *"His art of playing the harpsichord and the piano is beyond description,"* one of his contemporaries wrote.

The next point of interest for a tourist in Vienna is the 18th-century building where "academies", as musical concerts were called in Mozart's time, were regularly held. Mozart often took part in them. His recitals, which invariably drew enthusiastic crowds of his admirers, usually included an improvisation on a theme offered by listeners and a piano concerto, which was often composed specially for the next "academy." Since such events were fairly

Harpsichord by Benoist Stehlin, Paris, 1760 (Smithsonian Institution). The outer case decoration and Louis XVI stand are typical of the French treatment of instrument case and furniture design.

frequent, Mozart sometimes had to write a concerto within record time. It is known that once he composed two concertos within a week.

The Viennese looked forward to the performance of each concerto with great impatience. Indeed, Mozart's concertos for piano differed essentially from earlier works in this genre. The piano was no longer just one of the instruments of an ensemble which had a more extended part to play. Now the listeners heard an intensive dialogue between the piano and the orchestra based on a contrast between the solo and orchestral parts. The first and third movements of a concerto, were crowned with cadenzas, virtuoso improvisations performed by a soloist on themes from the relevant movement, allowing him to display his inventiveness and fantasy.

At the "academies" Mozart usually completed his performance with free improvisations, which a listener described in this phrase: *"He who has never heard Mozart improvising on the clavier cannot have the faintest idea of what he has achieved here."*

The great musician died when he was not yet thirty-six. But how much wonderful music he had composed during his short life! More than twenty piano concertos, of which seventeen were written in Vienna. Mozart's piano music, however, is not limited to concertos alone. The greater part of his heritage consists of sonatas.

Late 19th century decorated grand piano.

Listening to Mozart's sonatas, one may feel that they are very much like those of Haydn. Indeed, both composers used the genre of sonata and some features of their musical language have much in common: very clear, "transparent" sounds, at times resembling the sounds of an orchestra, and many of their sonatas are pervaded with the joy of life, sense of humor and subtle lyricism.

Both Mozart and Haydn were brilliant musical dramatists. Listening to the themes of their sonatas, one may often visualize operatic personages; in other words, the images evoked in their keyboard pieces are just as vivid and clear-cut as stage characters. This may be the reason why Haydn's and Mozart's piano music, so colorful, melodious and harmonious, is so easily comprehended by adults and teenagers alike. Two centuries after the death of these two great Viennese classics it captivates listeners as much as it did in their lifetime.

Shortly before his death, Mozart was visited by a youth of sixteen, and listened to his long improvisations. *"Mark my words. This young man will make the world talk about him some day,"* Mozart said after the boy had left.

That was Ludwig van Beethoven.

At the age of seventeen, Beethoven, dissatisfied with his life in his native town of Bonn, came to Vienna for the first time. Five years later, a year after Mozart's death, he settled in Vienna, though he hardly supposed that he would spend the rest of his life there.

In Bonn he had won wide renown as a brilliant pianist and improviser. In Vienna, however, it was far more difficult to gain popularity with the public, especially with its aristocratic audiences. His pianistic style was quite unlike the "elegant and brilliant" playing style admired by Viennese music lovers. As his listeners reminisced, Beethoven's manner of playing the piano was virile and profoundly sincere and had nothing of the impeccable filigree daintiness of Vienna's fashionable virtuosos. As evidenced by the well-known pianist Karl Czerny, who was Beethoven's pupil, his playing was *"inspired and majestic, as well as extremely emotional and romantic, particularly in adagio. His performance and his compositions presented musical scenes of superior vividness..."*

Whereas Haydn and Mozart had sometimes used the harpsichord in their music, Beethoven invariably preferred the piano, particularly in his mature period. He was a virtuoso pianist and constantly sought to improve this instrument. His opinion was heeded by Vienna's leading piano makers. On his insistent recommendations they imparted greater virility and forcefulness to the sounding of their instruments, that is, the qualities so pronounced in Beethoven's own art.

Beethoven's piano sonatas open a world of emotions before a listener. Sadness and the delight of triumph, violent passion and tranquil happiness -- the full gamut of human feelings -- are expressed in these works.

As is claimed by musicians, Beethoven's sonatas alone are enough to give eternal life to the piano, even if all piano music composed in other genres had never existed.

For all the beauty of Mozart's sonatas, his own attitude to their composition was far less serious than his work in the genres of opera and symphony. The same holds true of Haydn:

The "Presidential" Steinway grand piano, New York, 1903 (Smithsonian Institution). This instrument, the 100,000th made by Steinway and Sons, was used at the White House from 1903 until 1938, when it was replaced by the 300,000th Steinway, another specially-designed model.

the focus of his art was in chamber music and symphony rather than the piano music. Beethoven's piano sonatas, however, are the culmination of his intense creative quests, as in his chamber and symphonic music. Each of his sonatas was another step forward, another discovery in exploring the potentials of the piano for conveying the most delicate nuances of human feelings.

In his work on the formidable task of revealing in his piano sonatas the spiritual world of man, the world of human passions and emotional experiences Beethoven searched for new forms of expressions, exploring untrodden paths in music. The composer's musical language became more eloquent and forceful. His compositions grew to enormous proportions. For instance, the first movement of his celebrated "Appassionata" is longer than many of Haydn's sonatas. These are truly vast canvases, or, as his pupil Karl Czerny put it, "musical scenes."

And today, too, a century and a half since their creation, the performance of any of Beethoven's sonatas is a gruelling test for a pianist.

We recall this at Heiligenstadt, a little town outside Vienna in Beethoven's time, which has now been absorbed by the Austrian capital. Its long name is now familiar to music lovers around the world as a place associated with the name of the great German composer. We can see a monument to Beethoven here, visit the small house where he lived, and take a stroll along the alley bearing his name...

Fortepiano by Jean-Louis Dulcken, Munich, from around 1795 (Smithsonian Institution). The five-octave range of this late-18th-century grand piano suits perfectly the music of Mozart, Haydn, and early Beethoven, composed for similar instruments.

English double-manual harpsichord by Burkat Shudi, London, ca. 1743 (Smithsonian Institution). The registers are controlled by the brass knobs visible above the keyboards. The instrument's burl walnut veneer and turned trestle stand reflect English furniture of the period. The key coverings are ebony and ivory.

Now we have come to the end of our short tour of the musical sights of Vienna, a city which Mozart once described in this phrase: *"This is, of course, a piano wonderland!"*

Unfortunately, we shall not find a piano that belonged to Haydn, Mozart or Beethoven in any of the numerous museums of Vienna. After his death, Beethoven's piano, for instance, was bought for a song by a second-hand dealer and its further fate is unknown.

Now let us see what the piano looked like in Beethoven's time.

The 1794 Broadwood grand piano. The case is veneered, as was typical for English harpsichords and fortepianos. The two pedals perform functions similar to those of the modern grand.

7. THE GRAND PIANO

Whereas formerly the organ had been named as the "king" of musical instruments and then the harpsichord had reigned supreme for a long time, now the piano, or rather the wing-shaped grand piano, was in power. Thus, there was a change of government in the musical world.

The grand piano began to "rule the waves" in the ocean of music. Now composers and performing musicians reposed their hopes in it. It was expected to meet the demand of the vastly increased audiences for greater listening pleasure.

Mozart, who is justly called the first great artist of the piano, was passionately in love with it. He was delighted by every new improvement in its design and took advantage of it in his compositions.

As one of his friends testified, Mozart had a pedal keyboard made for his piano. This interesting fact indicates that the search for new expressive possibilities of the piano was pursued in different directions. In the abovementioned case it was provided with a pedals characteristic of the organ. Although Mozart willingly used it in his compositions, as students of his art testify, this device has not survived in the piano. The same fate befell many other ingenious mechanisms and contraptions used in the early pianos: "lute" and "bassoon" stops which were to provide a wider color range of the instrument a foot-driven device imitating the sounds of percussion instruments, and a host of others.

At that time neither musicians nor instrument makers could know that the distinctive qualities of the piano would be secured not by using imitative devices but by its own distinctive design which was yet to be finalized. The most important of these distinctions was the singing voice of the piano in contrast to the organ or the harpsichord.

Beethoven regarded this quality of the piano as one of critical significance. In his letter to a friend, the remarkable piano maker Streicher, he writes: *"It is a pleasure to know that you are one of the select few who understand and feel that the piano can sing."*

In Beethoven's day the piano was already in general use, so much so that scores of instrument makers in Italy, Germany, France, and Britain were steadily at work to improve it. Since, as we know, the idea of a keyboard instrument in which sound was to be elicited by a hammer striking a string had occurred to a few inventors practically at the same time, the mechanisms of the pianos made in different countries differed from one another. There were the "English" mechanisms which had their prototype in Cristofori's instrument and the "Viennese" mechanisms descended from Schröter's model.

However different the pianos made in London or Vienna, Paris or Rome might be in design, instrument makers were plagued by the same problems, so once a solution was found to any of them it was immediately applied by other factories.

One of the worst nuisances, for instance, was the low sound "ceiling" of the piano. Whereas a century ago the pleasant but much too quiet tone of the harpsichord had delighted musicians and listeners alike, in the 19th century the grand piano which was taking over not only salons but also large halls was clearly in need of more volume.

It seemed easy to increase the volume; one only had to make the strings thicker, longer and with more tension. When this was done, however, the wooden frame of the grand piano almost cracked. Indeed, the tension of the strings came to several thousand pounds.

Over the course of the 19th century, a way out of this predicament was found. As it had often happened before, metal gave a helping hand to wood. The rigidity of the body was secured by a cast iron frame, which made it possible to increase the tension of the strings to twenty-odd tons. By the end of the century, the strings were arranged crosswise in two tiers. This allowed the bass strings to be made longer, while the length of the piano remained unchanged. As a result, its tone became more brilliant, richer and louder.

Another important problem that worried musicians was the sound quality of the piano. Since the time of Bartolomeo Cristofori its hammers were coated with leather, which was cheap material but too stiff and not durable enough. After a period of use the leather on the hammer points striking the strings hardened, and sounds that were initially "dry" and devoid of rich colors as it was became even less melodious.

Various materials were tested to replace leather. Pressed felt proved to be the most satisfactory. A felt-coated hammer gave pianists unexpected opportunities for achieving various nuances of sound. As is claimed by pianists, this is what can make the sound of a piano dense or transparent, sharp or mild, lucid or dull.

These remarkable improvements, however, failed to satisfy instrument makers and musicians, especially virtuoso pianists who sought to identify the technical possibilities of the piano and make the most of them.

To repeat a note it was necessary to release the key to let it come back to its initial position. It was at this moment, however brief, that the pianist lost precious time. If the pianist pressed the key again too early when it had not yet risen to its limit the instrument failed to sound. This formidable problem which had caused headaches to many piano mechanics was solved by the talented French master Sébastien Érard, who came up with a new design of the piano mechanism in 1823. He called his invention the double escapement, and later it came to be known as the double-action striking mechanism. It permitted rapid repetition of a tone without raising the key to the limit.

Now the mechanism of the grand piano was quite close to its modern design.

This, however, holds true of the grand piano but not of the piano in general. Indeed, the grand piano was not the only representative of the young family of pianos. Indispensable on a concert stage or in a large hall, it seemed too cumbersome at home and took up too much space. True, there were pianos of other shapes, for instance, table-like models for the home but their sonority could not stand comparison with that of the grand piano.

The creative quests of instrument makers were never at a standstill. With the same persistence with which they perfected the grand piano they started designing a piano convenient for the home. Finally, they built an upright piano. Its prototypes were the "giraffe" and the "pyramidal" pianos in which the strings were arranged vertically.

True, first samples of the upright piano were quite unlike what it is today.

Every piano factory -- and there were a few dozen of them in the early 19th century -- offered its own models and its own innovations. Some manufacturers eager to excel their rivals made very exotic improvements in their models. There appeared a piano with rattle-boxes attached to it, which added noises to the normal piano tones. A piano of another factory had a violin-shaped resonance box. Its designers believed that to be a good way to lend a more melodious tone to the instrument.

Pianos were built in a wide variety of shapes and sizes. One could hardly find two identical pianos among those produced by different manufacturers. Just as the harpsichords had been made to imitate the furniture style of their time, the finish of both the upright and grand pianos matched the style of workmanship of furniture in vogue in the 19th and then in the 20th century.

Grand pianos varied in size from giants to dwarfs. In time they came to be classified according to size. The largest concert grand pianos measure over nine feet in length, salon models, up to seven feet, and baby grand pianos, about five feet.

Thus, masters who had worked persistently to improve the piano had good reason to feel satisfied: in the early 19th century the piano became the most popular musical instrument on the concert stage and at home.

However, the success of the new instrument was yet to be reinforced by the arrival of new geniuses of music -- composers and performers -- who would reveal in full the truly enormous potentialities of the piano.

The action from a Broadwood grand piano, London, 1794 (Smithsonian Institution): the strings are struck from below by leather-covered hammers. The late-18th-century English action is the ancestor of that most used today.

8. THE POETS OF THE PIANO

It is a pity that musical instruments cannot speak the language of words. They have a lot of interesting things to tell. Each of them has a life story of its own, which may be great and brilliant or quite uneventful.

Take, for instance, the story of a piano which had the good fortune to be owned by a great composer who revealed the poetical soul and vocal gift of the piano.

It is silent today, but there was a time when its sounds were heard almost daily as the genius who played it poured his heart out in melodies, harmonies, and intricate rhythmic patterns.

There is a small brown grand piano on bowlegs that belonged to the brilliant German composer Robert Schumann. It was the first to learn his impatient thoughts and express in sounds the constellation of harmonies brought forth by his fervid imagination.

It probably remembers young Robert's cherished dream of becoming a pianist and how he injured his hand by overwork at the piano, trying to gain time and make his dream come true sooner than it was physically possible. He had to give up his plans to have a career as a pianist. The gifted and stubborn youth, however, did not abandon his favorite art. He devoted himself to composition and achieved worldwide renown in this field.

Schumann's piano works are much admired by youngsters and adult musicians alike. It is not unlikely that the grand piano, which is carefully preserved at the Schumann memorial museum in his native town of Zwickau in Germany, was precisely the one he used in composing his *"Album for the Young"*, a collection of piano pieces for beginners.

Anyone who is willing to study or listen to these pieces is sure to have many fascinating moments of pleasure and discovery of beautiful music. On its pages one can meet with "The Brave Horseman," "The Poor Orphan," "The Merry Peasant," and "Santa Claus." The *"Album"* features songs under a variety of titles: "A War Song," "A Reapers Song," "A Sicilian Song," "A Northern Song," "A Village Song," and "A Sailors' Song," to mention but a few. There is a total of forty pieces in the *"Album for the Young."* Before the young pianist begins to learn these pieces he is obliged to read *"The Rules of Life and Useful Hints to Young Musicians"* with which Schumann opens his *"Album"*. Here are some of them:

"Among your colleagues make friends with those who know you better.

"There are many different people on earth. You ought to be modest. You have not yet discovered or invented what was not discovered or invented before you. But if you have been fortunate to make a discovery you should consider it common property.

"You should study life in all its aspects, as well as other arts and sciences..."

There is another surviving piano of the past that is a mute witness of creative quests and brilliant discoveries. It belonged to Frédéric Francois Chopin and is now displayed at his birth place, the small Polish town of Zeljazowa Wolja near Warsaw.

Chopin was a veritable "poet of the piano," as he is sometimes called by musicians. Many describe him as the greatest genius of piano music and say that it is hard to tell whether the piano was made for Chopin or Chopin was made for the piano. They were made for each other -- that may be the right answer.

A very modern painting of Chopin.

Today piano music is inconceivable without Chopin's preludes and études, nocturnes, waltzes, polonaises, ballades, and mazurkas -- his art as a whole.

Chopin was the first and, for a long time, the only composer writing music almost exclusively for the piano. In his wonderful compositions and in his playing this familiar instrument suddenly sounded in a perfectly new way. *"Listening to Chopin's playing,"* one of his contemporaries reminisced, *"many great pianists and composers saw new horizons in piano music and decided to follow the trail blazed by this young Pole, who heralded the future of the piano by his style of performance and in composition."*

Chopin's innovativeness is strikingly obvious on comparing works in the same genre produced by him and other composers, his predecessors and contemporaries.

Take, for instance, the *étude*. *A piano piece known as étude* was formerly intended exclusively for exercise to develop finger dexterity and velocity, and to secure the fluency of sounds, in other words, to perfect pianistic technique. Carl Czerny's *études* are an example in point.

Chopin's *études*, however, are a different story. Although most of his twenty-seven *études* require great mastery on the part of the pianist, their chief merit is their artistic message.

Chopin left Poland as a young man and never revisited his homeland. He was active in France where he learned of the tragic events following the November revolution of 1830 in Poland. The defeat of the Polish freedom fighters was a severe shock to Chopin. Under the direct impression of these events he composed his famous étude in C minor known as *"Revolutionary"* today.

Also at that time he composed the dramatic prelude in D minor, which made part of the cycle of twenty-four preludes so much favored by pianists. The music of Chopin's preludes is so expressive that it evokes vivid, almost visible images in the listener's mind. Take, for example, his prelude in C minor. It has only twelve bars. But what profound emotions and tragedy it conveys! There is a story that Chopin composed it when he saw a funeral procession slowly passing his house. Listening to this heart-rending music one seems to see a hearse followed by mourners appear at the beginning of a street and slowly approach the listener and then fade out of sight in the distance. Nobody can remain indifferent to this music.

Chopin's *études* and preludes are miniature pieces pervaded with poetry. This is equally true of his ballades, which were inspired, as his biographers believe, by concrete literary works -- ballades his friend, the Polish poet Adam Mickiewicz. It will be recalled that Chopin pioneered the ballade genre in piano music.

Chopin's mazurkas, polonaises, and waltzes are also very expressive, and his larger works, such as sonatas and concertos, present him, as one of his contemporaries wrote, as *"an inspired lyricist, an incomparable poet of the piano who elicited from it a rich gamut of feelings and moods, gentle, pensive, melancholy, or lucid."*

Frederic Chopin was called *"the spirit of the piano."* He lived a short but illustrious life, which illumined the future destiny of the piano with the genius of his art.

...There is a piano that would never venture a word, even if all other pianos learned to speak by some magic. Its silent keys are enchanted by their memory of the divine touch of the fingers of Franz Liszt, the greatest magician of the piano, now light as a puff of air, now swift as a hurricane.

Liszt's brilliant talent became manifest at a very young age. He was not yet eight when he gave his first recital. A year later he performed in public a sophisticated piano concerto by Ferdinand Ries, a pupil of Beethoven, and freely improvised on a theme of popular melodies.

That début took place in the Hungarian town of Sopron not far from his birthplace. After a short time his name became famous throughout Europe. At twelve Liszt was a sensational success in Vienna, and he remembered his first concert there as long as he lived. It was attended by Beethoven, who immediately appreciated the boy's phenomenal endowments. After the concert, to the stormy applause of the audience, Beethoven came on the stage and kissed him. That was a gesture symbolizing the continuity of the art of the greatest pianists.

Liszt was twenty and was already called "the King of Pianists" and "the world's best virtuoso" when he heard the playing of Paganini for the first time. He was stunned by the fantastic skill of the Italian violinist and described it as "supernatural" and a "miracle." *"If Paganini can make his little frail four-stringed instrument erupt such passages, I wonder what can be achieved on the piano?"*

Now this idea firmly gripped his mind. He devoted long hours to his work at the piano. *"...My mind and my fingers are working like galley slaves,"* Liszt wrote in a letter to a friend.

He sought to bring his pianistic skill to consummation but he was least of all concerned with his own fame. He regarded virtuosity as a means of conveying an idea, a message rather than an end in itself. *"To kindle and sustain in the soul admiration for beauty so closely*

A modern painting of Ludwig van Beethoven.

related to goodness" is one of the main aims that in Liszt's idea should be pursued by a genuine artist of the piano. Under the influence of Paganini, Liszt brought his amazing technical skill to a pinnacle of artistry and composed works whose sophistication was without precedent in piano music, such as his *études* after Paganini's capriccios, the *"Études for Transcendental Execution"* and *"Hungarian Rhapsodies."* That, however, was not his eventual goal, and he went ahead with his work on pianistic technique.

He employed his superlative technique to accomplish a task of unheard-of proportions, to translate the finest orchestral and vocal compositions into the language of piano. This gave birth to his famous transcriptions of Beethoven's and Berlioz's symphonies, fragments of Verdi's and Rossini's operas, and Schubert's songs. Now the piano could sing like a human voice, sound like a complete orchestra, and convey the complex orchestral-vocal pattern of an opera. Listening to Liszt's piano transcriptions, one can clearly understand what the great Hungarian pianist and composer had in mind: there is no music that could not be played on the piano; that truly universal instrument.

Liszt was a composer, a teacher of piano music, a musicologist who wrote a wonderful book about Chopin, and a performing musician. To play the piano like Liszt did; is it not the secret dream of any pianist, young or old? Few, however, have made this dream come true and achieved a comparable skill.

It was only once that talk of a "second Liszt" spread through the musical world. Some even expressed their preference for the pianist whose titanic exploit was unequalled in the history of music. It was all the more surprising that he lived in a country which had never been famous for its pianists.

A pair of photos of Franz Liszt, taken at different times in his life.

9. THE PERFECT INSTRUMENT

Now we have become familiar with the long and eventful history of the piano. We know of the popularity it has gained in the 19th and 20th centuries and its gradual changes in design.

Let us take a closer look at the modern grand piano.

It is best to begin with the keyboard situated in its broader part. A modern concert grand piano features 88 keys, of which 51 are white and 37 black. They are divided into seven-odd octaves. To the right of the pianist sitting at the keyboard is the treble, to the left is the bass. Instruments intended for the home have a slightly smaller keyboard: the last octave in the treble is incomplete. It will be recalled that the range of the piano for which Mozart and Haydn composed their music and Beethoven wrote his first compositions was not wider than five octaves. The keyboard is protected against dust with a fall-board shaped to serve its purpose. In the 18th-century harpsichords this board was also of instructional significance: François Couperin believed, for instance, that a beginner should by no means play without a music teacher's guidance and hence advised the latter to keep the keyboard under lock and key!

Spinet by Thomas Hitchcock, London, ca. 1710 (Smithsonian Institution). This spinet, like the modern spinet piano, was especially popular in domestic use because of its compact size, simplicity, and relatively low cost.

This plan view of the Hitchcock shows why such instruments are often known as "leg of mutton" spinets.

Under the middle part of the keyboard there are usually two pedals mounted on special brackets. The right pedal controls the dampers resting on the strings. It may be relevant to recall the way this mechanism works. If the pianist depresses the right pedal at the moment of eliciting sound, the sound flows freely and dies down naturally. Returning the pedal to its initial position, the pianist instantly stops the sounding. The right pedal not only prolongs a sound if the key is depressed and links individual notes but also can be used to increase the volume of sound, however slightly.

This is done in the following way: when playing slow music (in a lively or fast excerpt no effect will be audible) the pressure on a key when sound begins to flow is followed by pressure on the right pedal to elicit a slight increase in sound intensity, or, as musicians call it, a "crescendo."

True, this effect can be achieved only by a very experienced pianist who has a keen ear for his own performance. It takes great skill to use the pedal effectively. Indeed, it can be depressed as far as it can go, thereby raising the dampers to the highest points above the strings, or just a little. The pianists call such gradations "halves" and "quarters" but they are practically impossible to measure precisely.

The left pedal lends to the sound a muffled, thick quality. Its use imparts special colors to piano music and, in combination with other playing techniques, produces remarkable sound effects. In musical notation the moment of depressing the left pedal is designated by the Italian expression "una corda," which means "one string." Its meaning explains the

The 1794 Broadwood in plan view. Because it lacks heavy iron framing, this early grand piano resembles its harpsichord predecessors much more closely than its later-19th-century piano descendants.

principle of operation of the left pedal mechanism in the grand piano. Every key of the middle and upper registers corresponds usually to three strings tuned in unison and struck simultaneously by one hammer when the left pedal is out of action. When the latter is depressed, however, the entire keyboard, with its hammer mechanism, is shifted to the right, so that the hammer can strike only one string. The tone will naturally be softer.

In the upright piano this mechanism is of a different design. When the left pedal is pushed, the entire hammer system draws closer to the strings. The hammers, which are now nearer the strings, strike them with less momentum.

The Chickering "cocked hat" piano in plan view. The triangular shape is easily seen, as are the braces of the metal frame.

Now let us examine the entrails of the piano. First, open the lid, which, incidentally, has an important function: reflecting sounds coming from the piano case, it directs them toward the listeners. This is why a grand piano is always set on a concert stage with its open lid facing the audience.

The grand piano case rests on three massive legs. It acts as a resonator and is made up of several layers of selected "resonant" wood varieties.

The case bottom is the sounding board, a horizontal wooden plate which is wing-shaped like the piano case. The sounding board has a large surface reflecting sound. The acoustical qualities of a grand piano largely depend on the state of its sounding board. The latter is made up of broad boards glued together edge to edge. A sharp change in temperature or humidity may cause cracks along the lines of junction.

The most important structural element of the modern grand piano is the frame, which is rigidly fixed to the piano case. The frame is usually of cast iron in one piece, since it has to resist very great tension. Steel is stronger than iron but is no good for the frame, because steel is a very "resonant" metal. Therefore, steel is ideal for making a tuning fork, an instrument that produces an almost pure tone of definite pitch when struck.

Over the broader side of the frame facing the keyboard are set the small metal tuning pins. Each pin has one end of a string wound around it. The other end has a loop put upon a metal pin set on the opposite side of the frame. The tuning pins protrude through the openings in the frame and are securely fixed to the wooden plank under the frame. A pin can be slightly turned by a strong effort. In this way, by turning the tuning pins in either direction, the grand piano is tuned.

The strings of the grand piano are made of steel. The strings for the tones in the lowest register are the longest and thickest of all. They are copperwound to lend them a low bass pitch. In the middle and upper registers the strings are thin and shorter as they come closer to higher-pitched notes. A short and thin string has not enough vibration energy, to use the language of physics. Therefore, it has to be trebled by setting three strings in front of each felt-coated hammer. The "chorus" of each note is tuned in unison.

The hammers are set under the strings and put in motion by an intricate lever mechanism linked with the keyboard and varying in construction with the particular system applied in the grand piano. Let us recall the "Viennese" and "English" piano actions in the previous discussions.

The type of construction affects the pianist's "feel" of the keyboard, which may be more or less "pliant" under his fingers, easing or hindering his performance. The hammers are made of flexible wood and have felt-covered heads. The felt coat prevents adhesion to the strings on striking and helps elicit a distinctive piano sound with its wide variety of nuances.

A grand piano by Chickering, Boston, 1857 (Smithsonian Institution). This experimental design is called a "cocked hat" because of its overall triangular shape.

A seven-octave Steinway grand piano, New York, 1857 (Smithsonian Institution). Its massive rosewood case is set off by a filigree music rack, an ornate pedal lyre, and shapely carved legs.

The felt-covered dampers rest on the strings, effectively stopping their vibration. As each key is depressed, its damper is lifted, allowing the relevant strings to vibrate.

Tuning a grand piano is a veritable art that requires great skill, absolute pitch and patience. Indeed, the grand piano has about 200 strings, and a tuner has to adjust each of them several times in succession.

So much for the design of the modern piano which has proved its dependability and convenience over the decades of its use.

Does this mean that further modification of the piano is unnecessary?

Of course not! It is not unlikely that perhaps a synthetic will come to replace felt some day. A special pedal may be invented to enable the pianist to increase sound volume without difficulty as a violinist or a singer does. The possibilities are virtually limitless.

One thing is clear: the piano music we love so much and the piano itself will certainly live on and bring a lot more listening pleasure to music lovers all over the world.

Top: Plan view of the 1857 Steinway showing the straight stringing from treble to bass. Bottom: Plan view of the "Paderewski" Steinway concert grand piano, New York, 1892 (Smithsonian Institution). The bass strings, running diagonally across the case, overlap the treble strings, and the metal frame has become much heavier. This is essentially the modern piano.

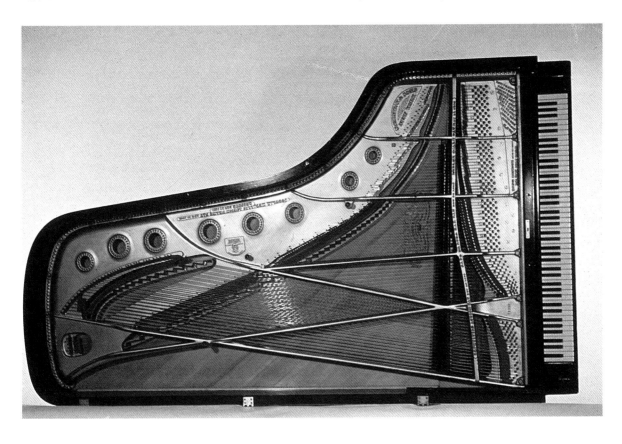

10. A SECOND LIFE OF THE HARPSICHORD

The harpsichord was forgotten for nearly a hundred years. The triumph of the piano was so spectacular that hardly anyone doubted that the harpsichord had gone forever.

It will be recalled that the harpsichord was viewed at the time as an imperfect predecessor of the piano. It was believed that the great 18th-century composers, such as Johann Sebastian Bach, Francois Couperin, and Domenico Scarlatti, and others of less renown, wrote music for the harpsichord, always having in mind some ideal keyboard instrument, one that has materialized in the piano.

This opinion, however, was not held by all musicians. Some enthusiastic admirers of ancient music came forward with a revival of the harpsichord as the best instrument for playing ancient clavier music. They pointed out quite reasonably that the piano, despite its rich sonority and variety of tones, was unable to convey the inimitable charm of compositions specially written for the harpsichord with a view to its distinctive tonal qualities.

A square piano by Zumpe and Buntebart, London, 1770 (Smithsonian Institution). This style of piano is directly descended from the clavichord, with the addition of a piano action.

An upright piano by John Broadwood, London, ca. 1815 (Smithsonian Institution).

Indeed, some compositions sounded far more effective when played on the harpsichord rather than on the piano, which failed to express some delicate nuances to make the overall impression of the music complete. This became obvious to the few musicians who were lucky to have found some surviving specimens of the harpsichord.

The problem of reviving the old instrument, however, proved a formidable one; even if some enthusiast had managed to discover a cembalo covered with a century-old coat of dust in a storeroom or a garret, it was invariably found unfit for use. So competent repair work and tuning were necessary to give the instrument a new lease on life.

An upright piano by John Isaac Hawkins, Philadelphia, 1801 (Smithsonian Institution). The portable design of this piano, complete with fold-up keyboard, so intrigued Thomas Jefferson that he ordered one.

The renewed interest in 16th-18th-century clavier music induced piano manufacturers to recall the long extinct art of making harpsichords. They came up against quite a few difficulties, since the secrets of the art, which had been passed on from father to son for generations, were now virtually lost. Small wonder, therefore, that the first harpsichords built in the early 20th century were by far inferior to their 18th-century models. That was all the more disappointing as the very same factories which had been famous for their superlative quality harpsichords before the advent of the piano now had to learn a new craft.

The first outstanding harpsichordist of the modern period was Wanda Landowska of Poland. Much of the credit for the return of the harpsichord to the concert stage is due to this energetic woman whose regular recitals in many European cities restored this instrument to its rightful place in music.

"Whoever has heard, if only once, Wanda Landowska's performance of J.S. Bach's "Italian Concerto" on a harpsichord will hardly agree it could be played on a modern grand piano equally well," an eyewitness wrote. A first-class pianist, Landowska often played the same works by old composers on both the piano and the harpsichord, so the listeners could judge for themselves which of them was better suited for a particular piece.

Landowska's many-sided activities as a harpsichordist and music teacher, as well as her interesting book "Ancient Music" awakened music lovers and composers to the beauty of the forgotten art. Manuel de Falla and Francois Poulenc, renowned 20th-century composers, dedicated their harpsichord concertos to the remarkable Polish musician.

Wanda Landowska's work has been continued by many musicians in the last few decades. Today harpsichordists are in a position to play ancient music on the variety of harpsichord for which it was composed. Works by English composers who wrote music for the virginal and by French composers for the clavecin are performed on the relevant instruments.

Some musicians have taken a liking to replicas of fortepianos claviers of the time of Mozart and Haydn, that is, the early prototypes of the modern grand piano. It is known that Mozart was fully satisfied with the tonal qualities of the hammer clavier, which was yet to incorporate the changes that would be made in the 19th century. It was precisely the instrument he wrote his music for. Indeed, listening to its delicate and soft sounds, one understands why it is best for playing compositions by the early Viennese classics -- Haydn and Mozart -- and some other composers. Take, for instance, Karl Philipp Emanuel Bach's "Concerto in E flat major" for harpsichord, fortepiano and orchestra. This brilliant composition was buried in oblivion for many decades. Why? The sounds of the modern piano are discordant with those of the harpsichord. However, hearing this work played in a duet with a fortepiano clavier makes the composer's conception perfectly clear: to show the difference between the two instruments and what they have in common.

The revival of ancient music is in evidence not only in solo performance. A harpsichord in an ensemble gives the listener much to admire.

A square piano by Chickering, Boston, 1850 (Smithsonian Institution). The simplicity in design of the earlier English and American piano cases has given way to a grander sense of scale and proportion, in keeping with the larger sound produced with the greater string tension possible with metal frames.

An upright ("Giraffe") piano by André Stein, Vienna, ca. 1810 (Smithsonian Institution). As in the modern upright piano, the Stein's strings extend to the floor, in contrast to those of the Broadwood upright, which stretch upwards from keyboard level. This piano's six pedals provide for special effects such as bells, drum, and bassoon stop, in addition to performing the usual functions.

Incidentally, some competent musicians believe that the violin agrees with the harpsichord much better than with the piano. Richard Wagner alleged that the piano and the violin are incompatible in principle. There were heated debates about J.S. Bach's six "Sonatas for Harpsichord and Violin." Those who shared Wagner's view insisted that these pieces should rule out the piano, since in composing them Bach had implied the likeness of the violin to the harpsichord as the underlying principle of their ensemble.

Today this view has been challenged by many musicians, and Bach's masterpieces are often played as piano and violin duets.

The harpsichord is indispensable in an ensemble with ancient instruments, such as the viola da gamba, the recorder, and others.

The cembalo (as the harpsichord is marked in a score) has regained a place of its own in the chamber orchestra as well.

An upright piano by Pleyel, Paris, ca. 1857-58. This fabulous example of mid-19th-century decorative design has a wonderfully-wrought case covered with tortoise shell enamel and brass, and candles to illuminate the music rack.

Just as in its heyday, the harpsichord today performs a wide range of roles as a soloist, a member of an ensemble, and an orchestral instrument, helping to bring works of old masters within reach of the modern audiences.

Of the two main types of ancient keyboard string instruments the clavichord has had a less fortunate destiny. Although it still attracts the interest of professional musicians and music lovers, its extremely quiet sound has proved an insurmountable obstacle to its appearance on the concert stage.

The life of the harpsichord would certainly not have been so illustrious, if it had been used to perform solely works of composers of the past. Although it is called "ancient" today, the harpsichord is an instrument of the present as much as of the past. As today's composers believe, its possibilities are far from being exhausted. New music is composed for it today to be performed along with works of the bygone centuries.

Keyboard view of the "Paderewski" Steinway.

11. THE PIANIST'S HARD WORK

We enter the festive and exciting atmosphere of a musical event. The hall is brightly lit with sparkling chandeliers. The grand piano is in the middle of the floodlit stage. Listeners smartly dressed for the occasion take their seats, and the murmur of voices gradually dies down to a hushed silence. Finally, the pianist comes on the stage and sits down at the piano. A moment of expectation, and then the sounds of music flow over the audience... Once the performance is over, the pianist is rewarded with applause, perhaps flowers, and thanks.

It is perhaps this festive atmosphere and the pianist's easy manner that makes some listeners think that it is very easy to play before the public. This, however, is a delusion of those totally ignorant of the pianist's hard work and of how difficult it is to become a genuine musician.

There is hardly another profession in which learning begins in early childhood and lasts for a lifetime. In this sense the profession of a pianist, as well as of other performing musicians, is unique. We can see from the biographies of outstanding pianists that all of them, with rare exceptions, started their hard work at the piano at a very early age.

Ignace Jan Paderewski's autograph inscription on the plate of the 1892 Steinway: "This piano has been played by me during the season 1892-1893 in seventy-five concerts."

Whenever a pianist's life was shaped in a way that precluded hard and regular study of pianistic technique in his childhood, he had to catch up on his training in his teens. That happened, for instance, to Sviatoslav Richter, one of the world's greatest pianists of today. He was not reputed to be a child prodigy and acquired his amazing pianistic skill during his term of study at the Moscow Conservatoire. Upon graduation, he went on with his training, to which he devoted a few hours every day.

How does a pianist work on a composition? There is a view common among the uninformed that a pianist learns to play a piece of music just like a reader learns a poem by heart. There is a similarity but only on the face of it.

A composer uses musical notation to commit his music to paper. This system of signs and symbols, however, is highly conventional. Composers have often complained of the flaws of musical notation that are a handicap to accurate expression of their ideas.

Franz Liszt writes, for instance: *"I have tried to explain my ideas by marking out precise instructions on music paper but I must admit my failure to express very much, perhaps the most essential of what I wanted to convey."*

A musician who is a true artist at heart must be able to read this most essential part of the music between the lines of the musical text and inspire a new life into its signs and symbols, as though recreating the composer's work in his own imaginative way. It was not fortuitous that Anton Rubinstein said that the performance of a musical composition is in fact its new creation.

What are the limits of a pianist's right to interpret a musical composition and his duty to its author?

A performing musician is not entitled to revise the rhythm or the melody and harmony of a piece of music. Even insignificant deviations from its tempo, however, which are quite permissible unless they run counter to the composer's conception, or slightly perceptible dynamic nuances, may change the character of a work substantially. Playing some part of a composition or the whole of it a little slower or faster, decelerating a bit the end of a musical phrase or accelerating its beginning, setting the balance between the melody and the accompaniment or between individual voices in a polyphonic composition, selecting a definite tone quality, are just a few of the many tasks handled by a pianist before a public performance.

It is very difficult to find the right measure in choosing among all these little options. Work on sound alone is a substantial problem to any pianist.

Piano sound... What makes it so charming and so hard to master? Indeed, it is a mystery a pianist works all his life to unravel.

When we say "lute," "cello," or "bassoon" timbre, we imply that each of these instruments, just as most of the others, has a distinctive tone color that lends a special quality to music played on them. In this respect piano sound is blank, that is, it can be filled with various timbre colors. Beethoven used to say that a pianist ought to master a tone color of his own. This means he is obliged to have his distinctive tonal palette varied enough to enable him to play works by different composers. Thus, a good pianist, just like a good actor, must have a gift for transformation and select special tone qualities for every composer.

Heinrich Neuhaus, a well-known Soviet pianist and music teacher, who taught, in particular, Sviatoslav Richter and Emil Gilels, is quoted as saying that *"the piano is the best actor among musical instruments, because it can play a wide variety of parts."*

A pianist's work on sound, however, is not an end in itself. Its primary object is to reveal the imagery of the piece of music to be performed. Tchaikovsky writes in this context: *"The central aim in playing a musical composition is to penetrate and explain, to the extent of one's talent and knowledge, the composer's hidden idea, which makes in fact the message of music. No task is more sophisticated and difficult than the one of expressing its meaning."*

The treble end of the action from the "Paderewski" Steinway showing one key depressed.

All great pianists of the past, no matter what individual traits they might have had, went out of their way to get a deep insight into the content of music and subtly express its poetic appeal.

"In his interpretations, Liszt attached first priority to the expression of the poetic idea," one of his contemporaries wrote. *"It was not an evenly sustained tempo or a regular flow of rhythms that determined his performance, but a musical idea and the content of motifs."*

A pianist who envied Anton Rubinstein's fame once remarked with annoyance: *"Isn't it unfair that the public forgives Rubinstein striking false notes by the dozens but none of such to me?"* It had probably never occurred to him that the public admired Rubinstein primarily for his meaningful rendition, the profundity of thought and feeling.

In our day when the average standard of pianism has risen spectacularly, professional pianists rarely strike false notes. However, listening at times to an impeccably rehearsed piece of music, in which all the notes seem to be in full accord with the composer's text, we inadvertently catch ourselves thinking that this playing is a bore and carries little appeal. Thus, as far as this aspect of pianism is concerned, the demands made on pianists, as well as on other performing musicians have not been eased. Today, too, a truly profound and meaningful interpretation is valued very much more than flawless playing devoid of passion and depth.

Needless to say, a meaningful rendition is a must not only to pianists but also to violinists, bassoonists, trumpeters, and others. A pianist, however, is confronted by greater problems stemming from the specific features of his instrument. One of them is the need to adapt to unfamiliar pianos.

"We pianists are worse off in this respect than violinists, who can very well keep their Stradivariuses, Guarneriuses, or Amatis, which gain more charm of tone as time goes on," the well-known pianist Emil Sauer writes. *"We are supposed to feel equally at home with a Steinway or a Bechstein, a Böesendorf or an Ibach, although they are quite unlike each other for both inner and outer design."*

A pianist is usually allowed to have one or two rehearsals to get accustomed to a strange piano. There is hardly enough time to check the alignment of the keys, and the tones of each register, since the basses, as pianists claim, may be "rich and mellow" or "dry and knocking," while the trebles may be "ringing and transparent," almost "crystal-clear" or "hollow and colorless."

The pedal also demands the pianist to accomodate himself to it. Indeed, every grand piano has a different pedal play. Unless he gets the feel of it, the pianist may press, say, the right damper pedal a trifle harder than necessary and smudge a musical phrase.

Adapting to the mechanical merits or demerits of the piano he is to play may be another problem facing the pianist confronting a gruelling test of his skill. Some pianos have a very pliant keyboard responding with a beautiful mellow tone to the slightest touch of a finger, while others may be so intractable that every note takes an effort to sound.

One must, indeed, be a master of his trade to learn to handle a strange instrument during a couple of rehearsals, if these are possible at all, with an artistry that makes every musical phrase a rich source of listening pleasure.

But mastery alone is not enough. In the phrase of the late Arthur Rubinstein, one of the greatest artists of the piano, the pianist must *"spill a few drops of fresh blood at every recital. Then he is a genuine artist."*

Irving Berlin's upright piano, made by Weser Brothers, New York, 1940 (Smithsonian Institution). The keyboard transposes a full chromatic octave, a device frequently found on pianos of Tin-Pan Alley composers, many of whom, like Berlin, played primarily on the black keys of the instrument.

THE PIANO IN RUSSIA

The musical season of 1885-86 in Europe was quite unlike any of the earlier seasons there. Music lovers were looking forward to it with great impatience. *"Fantastic! In only seven recitals one pianist alone will perform almost all piano works composed over the centuries!"* This news was hard to believe.

Bills announcing the historic recitals of the great Russian pianist Anton Rubinstein appeared in Europe's largest cities.

What kind of recitals they were is best described by Anton Rubinstein himself: *"It was my intention to present in a series of recitals in Europe's main musical centres, what might be called a review of the history of piano music. My plan was a total success... I gave seven recitals in each of the cities of St. Petersburg, Moscow, Vienna, Berlin, London, Paris, and Leipzig, and three recitals in both Dresden and Brussels. Moreover, in the first seven cities I repeated each of my historic recitals for the benefit of a select audience of music students assembled on the next evening. Thus I gave fourteen recitals in each of these cities. I was completely satisfied with my public reception and at all points of my guest tour I was greeted with general acclaim."*

Indeed, the pianist had ample reason to be pleased with his success, which surpassed all expectations. His triumph was largely due to his magnificent demonstration of the enormous wealth of piano music accumulated during the several centuries of the existence of keyboard stringed instruments -- the piano and its predecessors, and the great spiritual value of the piano and the music composed for it.

Another clue to his success, apart from the staggering number of works he had played, was the way he did it.

Here is an eyewitness account: *"When Rubinstein was at the piano, the audience was carried away by his emphatic personality. He seemed to be generating a powerful magnetic force, which made the listeners burst into applause before they realized it. He gained control over the audience in a forceful and resolute manner."*

His tour was an all-time record in pianistic knowledge, skill and endurance as yet not surpassed. His listeners saw an impressive scene of the past and present of piano music and performing art. The name of Anton Rubinstein is on a par with the world's greatest musicians if only because he did so much for the future of piano music. Today we often hear of international music contests held every year in many countries of the world. Few people know, however, that Anton Rubinstein organized the world's first international contest of young composers and pianists.

Rubinstein's contribution to the progress of Russian music was truly inestimable. It was on his initiative and to his energies that Russia's first Conservatory of Music was opened in 1862. Very soon this brainchild of Rubinstein's reached maturity and produced a brilliant constellation of composers. Among them three geniuses of Russian music were destined to play a crucial role in the future history of the piano.

...It's a frosty winter morning. The child has just awakened, and fragments of his night dreams are still alive in his memory. It's time to get out of bed not to lose an instant of the joyful day of games and fun that lies ahead. It may be best to start with playing a horseman, hopping about on a stick, which is an imagined steed. And here is Nanny, who is very kind but she may also be angry when he is too naughty.

Once he tries riding the stick, he becomes engrossed in playing with his toy soldiers, who draw up rank and march at his command, while he sounds a bugle with his lips. His favorite doll is not forgotten either. He is fond of dancing, so waltzes, mazurkas and polkas follow each other in rapid succession. But what can be better than a song, merry or wistful, slow or full of life?

It may be Italian or German, Neapolitan or Russian, or even an old French song; there are so many of them that a full day is not enough to sing them all before it's bedtime again. Nanny tells him a fairy-tale about the wicked witch Baba-Yaga, mischievous gnomes and good magicians and sings him a lullaby. As he falls asleep he seems to hear distant voices of a choir, the singing of a lark hovering in the air, or the sounds of a street-organ...

One may wonder why this story of a child's day should belong in a book about the piano. There is a good reason. It was written for children learning to play the piano by the great Russian composer Pyotr (Peter) Ilich Tchaikovsky. Even these tiny pages of his *"Album for the Young"* reveal the most fascinating features of his art: vivid melodies so easy to remember, and an amazing wealth of musical imagery.

Tchaikovsky loved the piano and willingly composed music for it. The composer of *Eugene Onegin* and *The Queen of Spades* and a host of wonderfully lyrical songs regarded the piano primarily as a singing instrument. He revealed the vocal properties of the piano in all his compositions with unusual mastery and ingenuity. Among the most famous ones are *The Seasons*.

These are twelve musical scenes corresponding to the twelve months of the year, which are charmingly lyrical impressions of Russian scenery. However, they are not simply musical landscapes but convey man's ever-changing moods influenced by the endless change of the seasons.

Each piece has the title of the relevant month and a subtitle. For instance, *January* is subtitled *By the Fireside*, October is subtitled *An Autumn Song*, and December is subtitled *Christmastide*. All the pieces are prefixed with epigraphs from Russian poetry. Tchaikovsky considered them very important for a faithful and sensitive interpretation by listeners. The music, however, is so expressive, captivating and easy to comprehend that even one unaware of their titles will sense their message unmistakably.

The performance of the pieces from *The Seasons* at the Tchaikovsky memorial museum at the composer's home town of Klin, a picturesque locality midway between Moscow and Leningrad, is an unforgettable experience. The privilege of playing them here is an honor granted to young laureates of the Tchaikovsky International Piano Contest held in Moscow every four years. When pieces from *The Seasons* are being played in the former drawing room of the composer's house, the sounds of music flow out of the open windows and float towards the distant copses and the picturesque banks of the river Sestra where Tchaikovsky loved to stroll, inventing the wonderful harmonies of these works.

The theme of Russian nature was equally conspicuous in the music of another Russian composer of genius, Sergei Vasilyevich Rachmaninoff.

He discovered new colors and discerned new subtle nuances of pianistic sound in the tonal palette of the long familiar piano, whose potentialities seemed to have been exhausted. Broad flowing melodies combined with Rachmaninoff's famous polyphonic chords, bring to life images never heard in piano music before. Inimitable church bell sounds and picturesque, almost visible glimpses of Russia lend a new and beautiful dimension to his compositions.

Sergei Rachmaninoff was indisputably one of the greatest pianists in the history of music. His finest merit was his imaginative interpretation of the work he was playing, be it his own or one of another composer. His thinking as a composer gave him his own vision of the music and lent it added richness of tone and depth of meaning. It was, in fact, a new composition. Therefore, it was equally fascinating to hear him play his own works and those of other composers.

The well-known Soviet authoress Marietta Shaginyan writes: "...*Though touring the country as a performing musician was hard work, Rachmaninoff was invariably at his best before any audience, even in an out-of-the-way small township with little musical life. He never relaxed at the piano. In fact, it did not matter much to him if he was alone or in front of a packed house;*

A detail of the Janko keyboard fitted to an upright piano by Decker Brothers, New York, ca. 1890 (Smithsonian Institution). The Janko keyboard was designed to facilitate playing of thickly-voiced chords of wide compass. Despite the establishment of Janko schools and the publication of methods designed to promote its use, the Janko keyboard never achieved widespread popularity, and was abandoned totally around the beginning of the 20th century.

once his hands were poised over the keyboard he felt a compulsion to create music, to bring it to consummation, to burn his heart out in the whirlwind of sounds. When the performance was over, he was down and out, his face was a gray mask of fatigue as he silently waited for his strength to come back."

Rachmaninoff the pianist and Rachmaninoff the composer were blended in an apotheosis of music.

There was yet another salient feature in his music. Using the composer B.V. Asafiev's pictorial phrase, it was "*the Russian instinct for the lyrical that manifested itself in the enchanting scenes of the majestic vastness of Russian landscapes, the quiet murmur and silent beauty of Russian forests and fields.*"

"The piano," Rachmaninoff said, *"is an instrument available to a wide range of amateurs, and it will always be in favor among them. The piano paves the road to a wider knowledge of musical literature. It is the best instrument for a beginner in the study of music."*

The art of Rachmaninoff the pianist and composer has been the epitome of pianistic artistry for many generations of musicians and music lovers. Indeed, the piano is a uniquely universal instrument capable of expressing the individuality and talent of any musician sensitive to the "soul" of the piano.

One such musician, whose career had started at the same time as Rachmaninoff's but proved markedly different from it, was Alexander Nikolayevich Scriabin.

Scriabin composed only piano music save for a few symphonic works. Like a science fiction writer he created an unreal world of fantasy in sounds from the piano.

Listeners were spellbound by this music, especially when Scriabin himself was at the piano. One of them recalls:*"...The gentle and alluring sounds of his music were inimitably beautiful. He was a magician who had perfect control of and a deep insight into the great mystery of sound. His pianissimos were full of charm... and his virtuoso pedalling enveloped these sounds in layers of some strange echoing undertones no other pianist could reproduce afterwards..."*

Scriabin had yet another amazing talent: he could form visual images of music inside his mind. That was a rare gift of color vision of sounds, and he dreamt of a piano that would produce an integrated sound and color picture, the play of colored light on a screen operated from the piano keyboard. Though he failed to make his idea come true, his music invariably creates a sensation of radiant light and soaring flight.

Thus, the piano became King of Musical Instruments; it was used to play symphonic and operatic music, to create musical portraits of human beings and scenes of nature, and to transport everyone to a distant fantastic world. Of all musical instruments, the piano alone is a perfect vehicle for expressing any shade of thought and emotion in the language of music.

THE EPILOGUE

Our story of the piano has come to an end. Now we know that ever since its invention in the early 18th century it has been steadily changed. What is more, the current century has seen the advent of electric keyboard musical instruments, which are superior to the piano in certain respects.

Does this mean that the piano is on the way out as an old-fashioned instrument retreating before innovation?

Of course not! The range of people eager to learn to play the piano is rapidly widening, and countless thousands of music lovers frequent concerts of piano music, listen to records, and never miss their favorite pianists' broadcast or telecast program.

The piano, with its amazingly rich variety of tonal colors and hues, is a beloved musical instrument as much as ever. It has long ceased to be an exclusive property of the aristocratic salons and has come within reach of the public at large. No other musical instrument is used so widely in our day-to-day life. It is a soloist or an accompanist, the most favored instrument at home, and an indispensable member of an orchestra of whatever size anywhere.

Playing the piano as an "inter-instrumental" musical language has become necessary to violinists and flutists, singers and cellists--in fact, to musicians of all specialities.

The wonderful music for the piano written by 20th-century composers -- Debussy, Ravel, Prokofiev, and Shostakovich -- just as the works of Beethoven, Chopin, and Rachmaninoff, expresses a rich gamut of human emotions and moods in the wealth of sounds produced by this unique musical instrument.

Centuries have passed since first keyboard instruments and first pianos came into being. But their magic is there, and its power never wanes as we can witness at every concert of piano music. The pianist appears on stage, sits down at the piano, and the audience is carried away by the sounds of music to the mysterious realm of melody, harmony, and rhythm.

Index

*dential" Steinway grand piano, New
903 (Smithsonian Institution). This
t, the 100,000th made by Steinway
as used at the White House from
1938, when it was replaced by the
einway, another specially-designed
model.*